The Eleventh Hour

The Eleventh Hour

Poems for the third Millennium

Kildare Dobbs

Mosiac Press
Oakville, ON — Buffalo, N.Y.

Canadian Cataloguing in Publication Data

Dobbs, Kildare, 1923–
The eleventh hour
Poems.
ISBN 0-88962-637-5
I. Title.
PS8507.035E43 1997   C811'.54   C97-930019-3
PR9199.3.D62E43 1997

Published by MOSAIC PRESS, P.O. Box 1032, Oakville, Ontario, L6J 5E9, Canada. Offices and warehouse at 1252 Speers Road, Units #1&2, Oakville, Ontario, L6L 5N9, Canada and Mosaic Press, 85 River Rock Drive, Suite 202, Buffalo, N.Y., 14207, USA.

MOSAIC PRESS, in Canada:
1252 Speers Road, Units
#1&2, Oakville, Ontario, L6L
5N9
Phone / Fax: (905) 825-2130
E-mail:
cp507@freenet.toronto.on.ca

MOSAIC PRESS, in the USA:
85 River Rock Drive, Suite
202, Buffalo, N.Y., 14207
Phone / Fax: 1-800-387-8992
E-mail:
cp507@freenet.toronto.on.ca

MOSAIC PRESS in the UK and Europe:
DRAKE INTERNATIONAL SERVICES
Market House, Market Place,
Deddington, Oxford. OX15 OSF

Mosaic Press acknowledges the assistance of the Canada Council, the Ontario Arts Council and the Dept. of Canadian Heritage, Government of Canada, for their support of our publishing programme.

For Asa Zatz

Contents

Preface

Part I

Invocation 13
The key 14
angel 15
Daylight... 16
Medaea 17
Paradise lost, etc. 19
The creation of Eve 20
Adam's curse 21
Apollo 22

Part II

The Three Graces 25
Coole.. 26
The big bang 27
The Quantum Theory 28
Passage tomb 29
Sleeper 30
Rome.. 31
Bicycles 32
Colours 34
The song 35
In praise of luck 36
The others 37
Mad girl.. 38
Ploughman 39
Ghosts 40
The unmoving motive 41
Jeffrey's place 42
Jeffrey's place, 2 43
Drive-in.. 44
Dr Parnassus' kaleidoscope 45
Berryman 46
Blaise Cendrars....................................... 47
Susanna and the Elders 48

Part III

Annunciation 53
Treason 54
Massacre of the innocents 55
Martyrdoms 56
The hour postponed 58
Elegy 59
Memorial 61

Part IV

On the fish war 67
On seeing a snake at Villa Epidaurus 68
Mortician 71
The invisibles 72
Summer cottage patriots 73
Saltspring Island 74
Immigrants 75
Bannerman reminisces 77
Dalmatian 78
Variations on a word 80
      1. The bridge 81
      2. At sea 82
      3. Tired 83
      4. A game of cards 84

Part V

Bombers 87
Dracula verses
      1. The governess 88
      2. The castle 89
      3. Dinner à deux 92
      4. Dead end 94
      5. Resolution 95

Part VI

Thanksgiving 99
The dear ruin 100
Enigma 101
Forgotten 102
O word of fear 103
Public appeal 104
Parting 105
The bionic woman 106
Safari 107
The cardinal at luncheon 108
Pilate washing his hands 109
Madam tells all 110
Perils and dangers 111
The road 112
Old man's song 113
Benediction 114

Preface

Readers who know my name, if they know me at all, probably think of me as an essayist, travel writer and jounalist. It may surprise them to have me appear, so late in life, as a poet.

The truth is I've always been a poet. My first poems were published in the *Kilkenny People* when I was fifteen. I was given early encouragement by John Betjeman, by the Irish poet Geoffrey Taylor, and by Peter Allt, co-editor of *The Variorum Yeats*. During the second world war I was published in *The Fleet Poetry Broadsheet*, South East Asia Command.

A long, dry spell followed the war.

In Canada my first literary venture was to broadcast my poems on CBC *Anthology*, encouraged by the novelist and screen-writer Charles Israel. I also wrote and performed in a travel show for television, produced by Ted Pope, centred in my poetry. Meanwhile my work began to appear in *The Canadian Forum*. My friend Ann Wilkinson showed some poems to A.J.M. Smith, who took one for his edition of *The Oxford Book of Canadian Verse*. Unwisely I also began to review poetry, angering some established figures, though I did make some friends too.

I continued making poems, placing a couple in *Saturday Night* and *Toronto Life* until, encouraged by Howard Engel, I broadcast another selection on *Anthology*, twenty-five years after the first.

The present volume is my first book, bringing together poems that result from a continuing impulse in later life.

A note on metre: the verses in this volume are hendecasyllables —an English version of the measure Catullus used. I favour metre because it allows chance to influence the poem. Syllabic metre is rare in English, though Marianne Moore made brilliant use of it. Tennyson wrote one small poem in hendacasyllables, marred because as a classicist he tried to introduce Latin "quantity", a system of long and short syllables that sounds unnatural in English.

In my own mind, poetry is the most important writing I do, the centre of my work and imagination. And at last I feel ready to publish it.

Part I

Invocation

illa cantat, nos tacemus

Come to me, you that in long silence I lost
Who sang to me in the orchards and hayfields
of the country of innocence, who changed me
with incurable wounds of intimation.
It was you I listened for in the voices
of children, of lovers, and did not know you.
You were the nightingale in the olive grove,
the larksong falling from sky over sand dunes
and the blackbird in the gardens of summer.
O come to me once more out of the shadows
in the majesty and flame of your singing.

The key

Think of a number, an odd number is best,
since that is truth itself, three in one or such.
All that's needed to touch the Absolute is
an arbitrary rule, like a line of verse.

angel

She that breathes life in this, muse or dark angel,
also brings death, an end and consummation.
Since it's too late for us, let the word go forth,
O let the word endure until icecaps melt
drowning the last cities and their libraries.
On the dark sea still let the songs be blowing
that shipwrecked sailors may hear and learn the tunes
and almost remember the lost happiness.

Daylight.

I have given up the oracles of night
for the mystery of transparent water

I have given up candles and enchantment
for the perplexities of clear afternoon

In this water I find time everlasting.
In this afternoon I discover my death.

Medaea

Peliaco quondam prognatae vertice pinus

Pines, so they say, from Pelion's peak once swam
through the sea-god's clear waters, surf of Phasis
to King Aietes' land, the good ship Argo
of evil destiny, groaned in the long swell.

Then, if ever, with their own eyes mortals saw
sea-nymphs start from the foam, bodies bare to breasts
exciting the men. But the golden fleece calls,
gold's desired more than seagirls, money than sex,
and Greek sailors know where there's wool there's a sheep.

With fishy girls these Argonauts want no truck,
they stink up the deck and are slippery cold.
Warm blood has more attraction, perfumed with thyme,
oregano, mint, sweet basil, all such herbs
as garnish the victim when men and gods dine,
yet can scent well the living sacrifice too.

As it happens, the captain captures a witch,
hot-blooded enough, yet boiling with evil.
and ever too ready to kill her own kin.

Sailors: they imagined evil as female,
and Medea was as nasty as could be,
the sort that cut your balls off in a divorce
and could not keep her nose out of men's affairs.
They should have ditched the black bitch in the dark waves.
Better to trust the ship, truth in her timbers,
and the sea too, Poseidon's kingdom of known
perils and dangers, the salt highway of trade
bringing gold-dust, honour and the clear road home.

Paradise lost, etc.

This is the garden, these its flowers and trees,
its gorgeous cockatoos, paradise birds,
heraldic leopard, gryphon, unicorn and
over here a wonderful talking python.
None of this is for keeps. Here by enchantment
a sorcerer has dreamed up his pleasure grounds.

One bite of the fruit of that tree clears the eyes,
disclosing a fever-ridden wilderness
and the poor tenants, naked and ignorant,
who signed the lease without reading the small print.
A bush fire set by the crooked magician
achieves an irreversible eviction.

Luckily the serpent, a grounded angel,
teaches all the arts of civilization,
including those of beginning and ending,
from which the man elaborates his own death
and the woman her tactics of renewal.
The new garden is seemlier than the first
and the terms of the lease more reasonable.

The creation of Eve

The man sleeps his first sleep propped on an elbow
beneath a vine; the lord bows down and probes
under the arm with analgesic finger
to bring forth the last creature of his impulse
and, as we think, the most beautiful of all.
Waking, the man beholds her, feeling the stab
of post-surgical pain by which he knows her,
and will always know her through generations.

The lord does not mention that he saw her first.
But the entire Old Testament will go by
before he chooses a woman he can trust.

Adam's curse

What if the sly father left a dying curse,
charging ingratitude, contempt unfilial,
what if brooding on his own unjust eclipse,
he wished his son better, yet still wished the worst?

What could the son do to avert the evil word
since, though unjust, it comes all too true at last?
Nothing. There is no reasoning with the dead,
and the evil that they write lives after them.

Apollo

I saw in my dream a woman at the turn
of the stairs above me, and with her a man:
the woman was my dark love who died in youth,
the man a shining stranger. I remember
he was a musician. He looked straight at me.
The glance of a god cannot be mistaken.

Part II

The Three Graces

These three naked beauties seem to be triplets
or one buxom woman from three points of view,

front, back and sides, but with different hair-does.
Full-blown roses playing at ring-a-rosy

they are surely not made for such exertion
but to hold still in the unchanging world of

reverie, reduced from three dimensions to
two by incantation of light and shadow.

We see the model for Raphael's Graces
turning stately in the Tuscan afternoon

and stately turning into the shadows of
the mortal dimension, the cold light of time

Coole

I walked in your garden, Lady Gregory,
where the poets strolled with you and carved their names
on the smoothboled beech-tree. You envied tenants
a secret locked in their faith and poverty.
Now your high walls that shut out famine protect
fat roses gone to seed, docks, nettles, fennel,
now blackbird and thrush whistle where Yeats intoned,
pensioner at your hospitable table,
who slept between sheets of Protestant linen
dreaming of long-haired girls in riding-breeches.
The big house ruined, sold up, bulldozed away,
himself lies buried in Drumcliffe churchyard with
the small gentry of Sligo that begot him.
Was that true civility, your world enclosed,
the soft light of candles in the dining room,
the talk and laughter of artists and poets?
Gun dogs and terriers snoring in the hearth
and the servant girls from the dank scullery
confessing Friday bacon to the curate?

Yet doing your duty in that state of life
to which it had pleased God to call you, I think
you as a clever lady must have wondered
did poetry and learning justify you

I am still of your race, Lady Gregory,
though I passed through the gates to far other worlds.
This ruined garden is our civility.

The big bang

Word reverberating over the abyss
before ever the light from darkness was severed,
before there was mind to instruct horizons
and father forth the colours of earth and sky
in the complexities of dying. Listen!
Nothing is lost, or everything; the sound
is gone out into the farthest galaxies
though sometimes I hear a rumour in my blood
like the intricate frenzy of a city.

The Quantum Theory

Einstein's response to the quantum theory
was religious, or at least aesthetic:
"God does not roll the dice with the universe."
But, professor, that may be what he does do.
No one else could have created laws of chance
and it's not hard to see why he'd do it.
Omnipotent and foreknowing everything
he must have lost all interest in his work
in the flash of creation, and so became
the great croupier spinning the nebulae
contriving crazy ways to surprise himself,
Allons, rien ne va plus! Les jeux sont faits!

Luck, not our freedom, puts God outside his work;
the great croupier is also peeping Tom
who happens to possess an all-seeing eye
and like sublunar voyeurs longs for a flash
of how things look when nobody is looking

Passage tomb

Like the words of an old song this stone, graven
with entoptic symbols, lozenges, spirals,
marks the door of a land otherwise hidden,

the country of youth or through the looking glass,
some say the fifth quarter of the four provinces,
and there beasts talk, the capons come ready-cooked,

no sun is seen by day, neither moon by night,
blood runs in the rivers and no one grows old.
Although it's not Eden, nor anything like,

heathen and believer meet there without fights.
People dying to get in, the stone remains
where fifty-five centuries hold it in place.

Sleeper

She sees him sleeping; surely, she thinks, he dreams,
and dreams of me. But just now his mind is dark.

Later he suffers visions of his last breath,
pinned helpless, deserted by lover and friends.

When his eyes open, wide aware he sees her
and for a moment wonders who she can be.

Rome

Tall, sunburned houses guard their shuttered secrets;
from baroque fantasies the pure element,
clear water, whispers in Bernini fountains.
In Gucci loafers, Levi-Strauss jeans, t-shirts,
elegant thieves step churchward to confession
where fathers sick of same old sins await them,
envying their jeans, their Guccis, their tight buns
and dreaming of olive groves in the far south.

Bicycles

The bicycle, though not sinful in itself,
(Drones the priest) may yet be th' instrument of sin.

Male and female created he them; they lean
Steel frame to frame against hedges, rails or gates,

Announcing pretty country folk at their play
In nearby ditches. Her thighs leap forth like trout

While joyously he rides her, gallop-a-trot!
And panting, gasping, Ah, she cries, don't stop!

The coloured fields fly by, then shadowed woodland
And sedgy water-meadows breathing wild mint

And river swans adrift on black pools and ponds
Till light and darkness clash in love's implosion.

Which sensing, Father Sly approaches tiptoe
And with stiff aspergillum casts aspersions –

Like Onan, wets the ground, like Cain, breeds blossoms
Priest after the order of Melchisidech

His conscience stings, yet holy nature triumphs.
The hazel groves let fall brown clustered filberts

The yellow fields astir with oats and barley
On hillsides hay grows tall and lush for mowing
Pied cattle laughing as they let down their milk.

The bicycles, all iron, shame holy church,
Handlebars sprout no flowers, chains no tendrils.
O brave machines that make the reverend sin!

Colours

Look at the sky, blue is the colour of light
as the masters knew who glazed the cathedrals.

Look at the fields, green is the colour of blood
and Jesse's blossoming rod bursting with leaves.

Look at the cows, red is the colour of beasts
and of seraphim singing beside the throne.

Look, look, look, the rainbow arched in the heaven,
the colours of an everliving promise.

The song

The song that invents the sun from black nothing,
the white moon from darkness, the garden from dust,
and spins from itself as the spider her tent
galaxies and planets, continents and seas,

seeks only a singer to sing, hymning forth
her One to scattered many, as the light breaks
on waters, splinters of sun-up or moon-fall,
each fiery sequin true original still.

In praise of luck

He hesitates, the distraught, the thrall of luck,
watching the dice, the cards, the wheel, the horses

all unaware of his own lucky chances,
first himself then all his bloodlines back to Eve

and beyond her have sidestepped many a setback
by chance alone, seldom by clever tactics.

Salt sea to slime to living cell to mammal,
who seized their chance when dinosaurs were destroyed

No super mind brought him to this dominance,
like so much else it was a matter of luck.

What is he doing here? He has no idea.
Yet being here, he has to invent his own game

and calls it justice, with arbitrary rules
that seem absolute. Also a god called Luck.

The others

O to be an arthropod, an arthropod,
an arthropod and wear all your bones outside!
Fittest survivors of them all, by the way:
whole nations of shrimps make a snack for a whale
yet it's whales that are endangered, never krill.
And what of lobster thermidor, forbidden
by Leviticus, nonetheless succulent?
In Davy Jones' Locker we grow rich and strange,
the mammal bones picked clean by lower orders.
Think of insects: the ever present housefly,
the cockroach thriving inside a reactor
and sugar ants colonizing the whole world.
Samuel Butler called stones our poor relations:
what shall we call these who inherit the earth?

Mad girl

They call me the crazy girl, mad as a brush
Flying all night long above the sleeping towns.
Below in the plane-trees the old king shivers,
Hunger, thirst and scalding cold his punishment
While free of the mundane gravity I rise,
Lit by celestial torches, Zion's beacons.

Joseph of Copertino, so they say, flew
By God's grace, and Sweeney flocks with migrant birds
Damned by Ronan's bell, book and righteous candle.
But I by the power and lift of the dream
Float in a Zodiac of undying love.

Ploughman

I can turn a horse and breast a horse to beat
The best in thirty-two counties. Thus boasted
The champion ploughman striding in his furrow
Followed by raucous birds, himself a sky man
Since he by night must plough up the Milky Way.
The burning coulter tugged by heaven's monsters
Goat, crab, bull, scorpion, lion, fish, in bright lights,
They're strong, says he, but give me an Irish horse

Ghosts

Sometimes I hear a child crying in the night,
other times an old man is lying in my bed
who looks at me and tries to speak, then fades.
From the street, a face at the window I see,
a fair youth looking out through bars and yawning.

The child crying, the old man, the prisoner,
I know them, they are my own, they are still here.

The unmoving motive

You could smell wild mint in the water meadows
where wild swans nested among flags and sedges,
where a child once ran no taller than the grass
and thought the wide river bed would always last.

Many deaths later the mint is fragrant still,
but the river swerves in another channel
and the swans have forgotten the way it fell.

The unmoving motive only man invents –
Invents or discovers, it makes no difference.

Jeffrey's place

Splinter of sunlight, jewel of summertime!

Precious among visitors to Jeffrey's place
who include, we believe, a decent sampling
of two-legged species from city and environs
(and some neighbours with four legs and bushy tails)
is *archilochus colubris*, gem of fire.

Missile of light, flashing metalic green shot
with crimson, darts and hovers at flowers
to suck sweet nectar, fuel for fiery blood,
the ruby-throated hummingbird no bigger
than a hawk-moth, his insect mimic, buzzes
fierce and swift, tiny wings a shadowy blur.

And when clouds over the lake chill the season
he's away two thousand miles to Panama
or maybe Mexico – we've seen him down there,
heard the strong humming of his bumblebee flight,
and there he's a god, spirit of fighting blood.

Now far from Tzintzuntzan, here in Ontario,
he probes at red flowers on a lawn by the lake
lighting the noon-hour and lazy afternoon
until at dusk fireflies blink their cold beacons.
And to this garden of brief sweltering heat
and lake all to soon to be ice-bound again –
he brings the equatorial flash and fever,
blossom of godfire in our dark latitude.

Jewel of summertime, splinter of sunlight!

Jeffrey's place, 2

The four-legged, bushy-tailed neighbours are foxes
who live in jungly cover at the bluffs' edge.

Moving gracefully in her famous foxtrot
in the hot afternoon, a vixen comes near

to the sun-warmed house for a handout of scraps,
provided by hospitable Genevieve.

Rambo the "harmless necessary" fatcat
sunning himself on the lawn is quite outraged,

this is his place, after all, its humans trained
by him alone, and after he chose them too.

Flat to the ground, with ears laid back, he shows rage
in every bristling whisker. To no avail;

the fox makes no never-mind, it's her place too.
Here she was born and right here she means to stay.

The pied fatcat may lash his tail all he likes
but she's going to eat up every morsel.

Drive-in

A trick of light sustains the clever conceit
of paved boulevards, the appearance of crowds,
towers, curtain walls, skyways, moving traffic.
Look. Look again. Nothing but poisonous swamps,
nothing but winged insects, bullfrogs, garter snakes,
bare acres disembowelled by bulldozers.
The deceiving screen can show a whole mountain,
or one bare breast climbed by a jewelled beetle,
or a web spread to catch lovers in their trance.

This plane of swaying shadows is all there is.
Look, her face is modelled out of illusion.
Surely this deception was dreamed by a god
to kill the tedium of reality.

Dr Parnassus' kaleidoscope

Doctor Parnassus has a kaleidoscope
that makes stars and flowers of the broken bits

of toy lovers, bright fragments he searches out
in garbage cans and basements. Look through this end,

some of this is from your attic: that blue glint,
intricately refracted and reflected,

is my right eye; that opening red rose is
a cross-section of my heart's left ventricle.

Who could guess that this shining geometry
is a chance arrangement of severed organs,

dismembered first, then disremembered? You are
surprised to find me beautiful after all.

Berryman

Stared at, fiery sun burns black: thinking too long
about god awakes his attendant horrors

Loneliness of your spirit solitary
after a day of students, women, whisky,

is not cause enough. There's lonely sadder far
when pain itself can be welcome company.

Sweet in your lens the dear earth of blues and green –
forget the maker, his work is all he is –

yet you yearned, it seems, toward the black wipe of
electroshock, the on-rushing shadow of –

for your father before you destroyed himself,
shooting his offence like a toxic culture

into your young brain to grow and poison hours
by hours. And the last unbearable minute.

Blaise Cendrars

Old sweat Cendrars, singing against the cafard,
world voyager drinking to steady the eye,
maybe we too could type straight from the bottle
while these fingers on the keys did the talking
if our days like yours were drilled by forced marches,
our nights locked in barrack-rooms and whorehouses.

It is my life I invent without design,
winging it like an old forgetful player
while the verse turns out to punctual bugles.
Soldier, you alone sing faultless in your freedom
as you march with your legionary's shuffle.
Those who come after you falter and stammer,
ignorant, too often, of your name and art.

Susanna and the Elders

How the masters loved to paint sweet Susanna,
stripped to the skin for a bath in her back yard!
A strapping woman with the legs of a wrestler
and breasts like musk melons, but also a prude,
or maybe just lacking in respect for age.
The two elders appear beyond reach of lust,
yet that lucent thigh is a provocation
hardly foreseen by the lawgiver Moses.
Nothing in Leviticus briefed them for this.

Too bad the lady is so single-minded,
intent on no more than the solitary
comforts of simple water and cleanliness

One old man a nice Jewish girl might go for,
if propositioned in style after the bath.
aroused by worshipping eyes to a thrill of
her own divinity and aptness for love.
But a double-header without such magic –
this is not Susanna's fancy at all. She
takes up a towel to eclipse her bosom,
a lady affronted in her own garden.

The jewel in her hair, the golden ewer,
sculptured cupids and dolphins in the shadows
and rich fabrics speak her exceptional worth.
Take care Susanna! accidents are common
in the bath or near it as statistics show
and the lives of many martyrs yet unborn –
Cecilia, for one, will face an ordeal
of scalding steam in her calidarium –

maybe to yield would be the lesser evil,
forego resistance, under the spurting fountain
whose dark waters will punish with deadly cold,
let God perform his own sarcastic judgment!

Not Susanna, whose bold ambition is
to star in scripture, if not in the canon
for doctrine, at least for edification
Apocryphal. So, Hosanna, Susanna!

Part III

Annunciation

Coition with a god not uncommonly
brings with it kinky security measures.
Chosen heroines are obliged to suffer
the hurried thrusts of a bull or a large bird
or ejaculations in showers of gold

A plain band on the third sinister finger,
even diamonds, might have proved better friends
for in spite of all precautions, there is talk.

The giver of laws has to make it legal
when he chooses one woman of his chosen:
minding the precedent of Leda's swan, he
sends his fiery sperm by carrier pigeon
escorted by a luminous messenger.
The lady is reading in her golden room
with marble floor and white lilies in a vase.
However polite and gorgeously arrayed,
the intrusion of this being is not welcome.
It folds its wings, proffers a flowering branch,
kneels and emits a Latin salutation.
Pouting, the maiden tugs her shawl around her.
Who is going to believe one word of this?

But when the holy visitant has vanished
she finds herself singing of liberation.

Treason

This is a picture that lives inside the eye
till the inventing lights vents it again:
the man broken, all crossed up on his high hill
stretched between gendering sky and mother rock,
arms stretched forever to horizons of night.

One thing is certain, there was a betrayal.
Witnesses heard him breathe the prophet's name, or
so they thought. But it was another he accused.
Looking for rescue in the turning shadows,
he saw instead the waters yearning for him.

No matter if he was some kind of monster,
by-blow of the winged air and earthly maiden;
so are all who suffer that final treason.

Massacre of the innocents

Killing a whole crowd of babies at once
was even more harshly repugnant to an age
accustomed to killing them one at a time
than to our own which hardly ever ventures
on single murders but glumly carries out
mass slaughter with the sanction of principle
or the declared wishes of the majority.

Butchery was hard work for Herod's soldiers,
though cheered, perhaps, by the joy of cruelty
and resentment of women and dependents.
For the king it was an act of policy,
regrettable, of course, but necessary.
The mothers cried a lot, but grief soon passes.
Before long, most of them were pregnant again.

All of which the painter has composed into
an exciting tableau in which the horror
is contained, becoming part of the beauty.
I do not know the moral of his story.

What I know is this: all was botched from the first,
darkness came in with light, with the best, the worst,
nor can it ever be mended hereafter.
What other remedy is there but laughter.

Martyrdoms

All I know of Sebastian is this
image of tranquillity under duress.
He seems anaesthetized by the ecstasy
of faith. With every vital organ punctured
he preserves his cool and even his colour.
Soldiers and spectators are in their best clothes,
the sun is donating holiday weather,
another great day for archery and Christ.

Relieving the sweetness of plump madonnas
with their stunned country faces and childish hands,
Eulalia's mastectomy brings a thrill
of sex and violence to sad piety.
Her breasts sit on the dish like pink *blancs manges*
while she stands butchered with the pained expression
of a woman who has missed her period.

So the monk, a meat axe sunk in his shaved skull,
suffers on with a look of mild annoyance
as though waiting his turn in the surgery.
Another is disagreeably surprised
To witness his own gut wound out on a spool.
A third frowns while roasting on a red hot grill –
glory will come when he is done on both sides.
And see where Tecla has been saved from drowning
for torments far more gruesome. She rejoices
to be hitched to ox teams and then torn apart.

Pictures are silent, one does not hear the screams,
let alone the buzz and chitchat of the crowd,
the bird song, buskers' music, creak of cartwheels.
The moment, arrested in dreadful stillness,
waits for the resolution of judgment day
when the losers win, and villains get their lumps.

The hour postponed

The hour postponed, the angel takes a raincheck
and next time will be worse than you imagined,
Not Bach's sweet hour with heavenly honey blessed,
not music's empire, nor harmony of the spheres,
but the last crunch of an inner universe,
ruin of time-space as the mirror splinters.

And of course the grave, where entropy's still law,
making a kind of dark music of its own,
and still the bright galaxies go blazing on
while leonids fall like the tears of heaven.

Elegy

In a flutter of ostrich feathers – white lace
softening the hauteur of bust and bustle –
Dublin virgins curtsy to fat King Edward.
One of that rare breed is my fair-haired mother
waltzing with red-faced cavalry subalterns
till my father carries her to Bulandshahr
and all the gay soldiers march away to die.
Carelessness, she claimed, brought forth her eight children,
and anyway even numbers came cheaper.
She loved solemn music and funny stories,
champagne, old brandy and astonishing hats.
Visitors would find her gentle, soft-spoken;
diverted by blue eyes and small stature
would miss the true steel of her temperament,
a woman not unlike one of her own cats,
sensuous and soft and afraid of nothing.
At sixty she began to play the organ,
at seventy took lessons in Irish harp.
Music almost reconciled her to Belfast
where she tuned her last crotchets to guns and bombs.

One summer afternoon in her frail eighties
a nurse takes her for a drive in the country.
They come at last to a great house by the sea;
she knows this place, the loud surf of long ago.
Through a door she sees her father and mother
and her youngest sister sitting together.
Her father smiles, but the two dead women frown,
shaking their heads, no, it is not yet her time.
Later the nurse brings her a nice cup of tea.

But where was her husband, where her young brother
killed at Gallipoli by a Turk's bullet?
Not for us to question such intimations.

Once more cherry trees bloom in the Malone Road,
fresh whitebait are frying in the restaurants
and girls in miniskirts moving among the flames
of Ulster's holy and undying angers.
She comes back to Dublin in her own good hour.
choirboys sing her hymn in the grey cathedral
for she is away on another journey
and almost certainly travelling first class.

Memorial

The day of Queen Victoria's funeral
in the sad ranks behold my Irish father
resting on his arms reversed with a downcast
mournful gaze, as the royal corpse expected.
The pipes lamenting, muffled drums, muted brass
and *The Times* grieving within sable margins.
Buttoned in creeds my patriotic father
strong for empire still hero-worshipped Parnell,
never once baulked at contrary opposites
and angry at English misrule in Ireland
took ship for India where, a sahib himself,
he served the Raj, and once had a witness slapped
because it was hot and the man was lying;
later in a train he arrested Ghandi
and thought no more of it, all in the day's work.
He also said the evils of our age
resulted from giving the vote to women.
Six fair-haired daughters arose to vote him down.

Long before the hour of his own leave-taking
in the seventy-ninth autumn of his age
where he lay like a weathered Irish ruin
choosing his own burial hymns, with the excuse,
"How else should a dying man amuse himself?"
Long before that hour,
with Ireland first, then India, gone to the dogs,

Big-boned as a dinosaur my father strode
tall in tweed breeches and starched collars which he
kept in a crocodile box on his brass bound
campaign chest, beside two silver backed brushes,
a tin of Brilliantine, his folding scissors,
a photograph of my mother (silver framed)
and a bottle of bay rum. In the quiet
of Kilkenny nights thieving age stole his sleep.
To lighten the smothering dark he'd whisper
Milton's *Lycidas*, learned by heart on purpose,
a sure soporific; but sleep brought nightmares.
We could not know what terrors made him cry out.
When his sight threatened to fail he shut his eyes
and blundered upstairs, impatient to be blind,
invoking Homer, Milton and Raftery,
sightless seers all, to light his way with words
("I Raftery, poet, full of hope and love –").
Light! yet he lived without electricity.
He hated telephones; as for motor cars,
he drove thirty miles an hour on the wrong side
(because that was his good eye) and still preferred
his Sunbeam bicycle, vintage nineteen-one.
He read the Waverley novels by lamplight,
wrote letters in the periods of Macaulay
and shouted edicts through his study window.

In a leather bound book he wrote names of friends
with notes of careers, honours, marriages, deaths
(but mostly deaths):
Sir Charles Kendall, judge, killed in an accident
on the road to Naini Tal, aged fifty-seven;
Francis Chamier, succumbed to cholera;
J.E.Goudge O.B.E., after eighty-eight
years of public service, private virtue and
a country walk, died in his chair by the fire.
Less lucky, G.Smyth, old schoolmate, was murdered
at the Cork County Club during the Bad Times.

F.A.Obeyesekere, however,
a Trinity Cambridge scholar, survived to
become speaker of the Ceylon Assembly.

Peace to the visiting friends of retirement,
old, honourable, talkative Dubliners
like this one, late of the Indian Railways,
noted stamp collector, with ill-fitting teeth;
or that one, author of *Hockey in Ireland*,
singer of Victorian songs on request,
my mother at the drawing-room piano.

In none too certain hope of resurrection,
my father chatted about law and the weather
repeating his story about the Rajput prince
("What, did you not know? He tried to poison me!")
The country people found him approachable.

Conscience, his mother's sour milk, choked ambition;
he retired early, side stepping the insults,
the trip wires of power, of art or action,
a conspicuous man afraid of notice –
yes, even his tombstone is illegible.
Yet I, a son whose birth he hailed with fireworks,
honouring my sire as per fifth commandment,
tune up my strings to mourn his ruined wishes.

Princes and powers fall to the blade of time,
their garlands withered and the last servant dead.
My father lies in Castlecomer churchyard
with Queen Victoria's coffin in his head.

Part IV

On the fish war

Come all ye brave Newfies and sing this refrain,
A finger in the eye for the pride of Spain!
Huzza for Tobin the Canadian champeen –
God help the fishermen and God Save the Queen!

On seeing a snake at Villa Epidaurus

Come hendecasyllables and do your stuff
we've sat here prosing by the sea long enough
and you, brown snake hips, old alphabet maker,
fork tongued double jointed insinuator,
as Cadmus I cite you, for so you were called
in antique stories before your blood ran cold –
come, bring back your sweet old fashioned ABC;
bring back, while you're at it, my bonny to me.

A god was born in this place, so they tell me,
patron of Osler, Bethune, Marcus Welby,
Banting, Best, Penfield, likewise Raymond Massey
as Doc Gillespie – all medical pashas.
That god too I hail in metre propitious,
old Asclepius with his Caduceus!
fix me a dose, old quack, to riddle-me-ree,
bring back with your snake and my bonheur to me.

Note the serpent theme common to both these stories,
a favorite tune in old Epidaurus.
One more legend that may have a bearing on
our thesis is that of Saint Hillarion
who burnt a dragon here for eating virgins
(a clean diet though the appetite was dirty.)
Burn for me, serpent fire, hilariously
and bring back my heart's warmth, my bonfire to me.

In a dream I tell all this to Northop Frye
who says, You've garbled the myth, I wonder why?
That serpent belongs in Paradise garden.
Right professor! says I, but beg your pardon,
what with ivy and thorns the place is a mess
I took this sacred grove for a wilderness.
Old snake hips and I plus the lost rib make three!
Then bring back the word and my bonny to me.

Three, three, the rivals! and possibly a scandal;
so in my dream I write next to Ann Landers.
Honey, she prints (qui mal y pense soit honi)
knock off this sick griping about your bonny!
and a snake's just a stick of type, Holy Moses!
trying to insert your column here for free!
So, jerk, go get fresh with your bonbon, not me!

But Moses did magic his rod to a snake,
then slugged up Sinai to cut shorthand on slate.
Take a commandment! Mister Thunderbolt booms
(Don't do it! ten times and then the Pentateuch.)
Sometimes Freud's cigar's just a cigar, agreed,
but snake's still phallus and holy glyph to me,
and letters are mail (dig?) to post in a slot,
and that's why I'm writing my bonny this lot.

Snake hips guards the precious thing hard to attain,
wisdom's hidden treasure for heroes to claim,
and the tree to be desired to make one wise
yields its sweet poisoned fruit only where he writhes,
lissom, articulate and with, so I'm told,
twin genital members, though sex leaves him cold.
Burnt, he fears the fire; and hides in his old tree.
Looks like there's no one in the garden but me.

Mortician

sees them exercising, no more cigarettes,
shunning the polyunsaturated fats,
riding a bike, wearing helmet and spandex,
obeying traffic signals and speed limits,
still hungry at table yet calling it quits,
fastening seatbelts, rejoicing in safe sex,
drinking only water, staying home Fridays,
reading feel-good books on the latest health craze.

Still they turn their toes up, brought for disposal
by sanitary means like fire or burial,
and many are prayed over, anthemed and psalmed,
and often like Pharoh himself, they're embalmed.

Then a slab, make it marble, carved with this text,
Here lies a denier of life. And you're next.

The invisibles

Pity the invisible majority,
the hidden hands, the faceless bureaucracies,
the moral multitudes, voices never heard,
smiles and faces you meet and quickly forget.

Like air, our element, they are everywhere,
colourless, odourless, even transparent.
Pity them? Yes, because everywhere's nowhere;
and everyman is no one anyone knows.

Summer cottage patriots

You like canoes let me make you a canoe,
a big one on a lake with a loon in it
with French-Canadian dwarves to paddle you
or city women got up as Indians,
also meself in a tall hat, the Bourgeois
no less! And a rainbow trout for our dinner
and any amount of fancy outdoor sex.

Unfortunately our canoe is leaking,
our lake polluted, our loon almost extinct,
our dwarves on strike again, our city women
demonstrating against menstruation and
someone stole my hat and poisoned our fish,
as for outdoor sex, you get sand in your seams.

Which is not to deny the force of landscape
as metaphor; or the reality of
history, the great river of Canada
draining the beaver meadows and moose pastures
and our forebears speaking with double entry.

The truth could be hard to bear with dignity.
The deprivation by which we inherit
is not ours to flaunt as a banner of pride.
Be content that we have done well out of it.

Saltspring Island

'This is a recycling island' where the sun,
often occult, is the sole permitted bleach

Not here the artifice of whiter than white.
What's adored is Nature, honoured with commerce,

The health-shop her temple, where pale vestals serve
City-bred fugitives from their own squalor.

Fog strays in firs, arbutus, yellow maple,
And there the bald eagle soars and stoops to kill

A fine place to visit. Yet even the birds,
Seasonal transients, winter in the south.

Immigrants

From the dark they came to this fine Canada
from the black abyss before our lives began,
and the first thing you know they're building a house
and you can't find a job, they've taken them all.
Like folks from out of town who, as you well know,
commit all the crimes—and especially rape
they elbow their way into the best places.
Next up, they're parading the streets with banners
and it's down with the country that let them in!
And the natives restless, the true-born bitching,
it's not good enough for us, we deserve better.

Love it or leave it, that's what we always say,
go back to the black abyss where you came from.
the snag being that it's where we all came from,
and where all, no matter who, go back at last.

You too started from dark beyond memory,
like it or not we're newcomers every one
infesting a land too vast to imagine
—time takes four leaps and a half to fly over—
furnished with farmstead, small town, high school, frame chur¢
necking in back-seats, blowjobs in the red barn
and the horrors of unforgiving winter.
And remember, there are spirits in the woods
and in the sky where dawn hangs out her banners;
monsters in rivers, lakes and estuaries
and the encroaching oceans. Still we bawl our hymns,
'His chariots of wrath the deep thunder-clouds form
And dark is his path on the wings of the storm.'
Looking about us briefly in the cities
invented by this clever generation
thronged with the world and his girl, the sturdy whores
shivering on sidewalks, the glazed accountants,
the walked-on grass, the municipal flower-beds,
we forget the brute fact of our going home,
back where we came from into the black abyss.

Bannerman reminisces

My first wife – did you ever see my first wife?
ah, but she was a beautiful woman!
Beautiful! and jumped in bed with anyone –
anyone who asked. She made me popular
I can tell you. I failed her; but after all
how could one keep such loveliness to oneself?

Dalmatian

When I come out with some trite observation,
making what's known as smalltalk to pass the time,
Vladimir says Of course! and I deserve it.
I notice how clear the Adriatic is
(of course) how lovely the Montenegrin girls
(of course) how the broom is golden along the
hillsides by the water, how the pines perfume
the lazy noon hours of sun and plum brandy,
how closed are the faces of the nuns (of course).
Of course communism is an empty bottle,
of course the leaders are larcenous old farts
and the newspapers lying of course (of course).

Flattered at first by emphatic agreement,
I do my damnedest to be more singular
by deploying my personal history
thus: I am Canadian, also Irish,
though born (adding the clincher) in India.
Vladimir says Of course! Do I deserve this?
Can there be any fact known only to me?
Any thought which this Slav has not thought before?
The CN Tower in Toronto, I scream,
is the world's tallest free-standing erection!
(Of course. Look in the Guinness Book of Records.)

Listen, I have devised a new theorem
not yet published in Nature or read to the
Royal Society to polite applause,
reconciling sub-atomic physics with
gay liberation, McLuhanism and the
product of half the number you first thought of:
quarks, queers, quibbles, quotient, Q.E.D. Of course.

Aurangzebe

This is the place, the last light leaking away
flashing from kingfisher's sapphire over pools,
Aurangzebe's tomb beyond, no Saracen dome,
but a mound of soil piled on the caravan
of cruel regrets, reasons of policy.
Balanced crosslegged on a water buffalo,
the slim boy lips his flute, a tune of moonrise.
Stop the car. The moment is now, forever.

Variations on a word

1. The bridge

Issa said, Life is a bridge. Build no houses but pass over.

This is the bridge between dark and darker still
and we have built no houses as we run on.
Hear this, we cross over the beautiful earth
where each townland's encountered once and for all,
the last time over and over, to the end.

Light up the last cigarette and say the prayer,
a bullet in the neck for this old joker
who built no mansions, owns no equity here.
And before you squeeze the trigger, grant this wish,
expedient or not. Tell him the whole truth.

2. At sea

From the bridge you can see far, even at night,
the whitecaps' commotion, wake's phosphorescence,
and close by, firefly glow of the binnacle.

Movement of dark on dark snags the alert eye.
Bearing red four oh, red four oh, dark object.
Looked at directly, the movement disappears;

Looked at sideways, it's there all right. Periscope?
A balk of timber, shark's fin, a sailor's corpse?
Look away, port lookout, to see it better.

Now red four five, square on the port beam, still there,
an oil drum recognized no longer threatens.
With luck we may survive this watch after all.

3. Tired

Fatigue: a silent bridge leading from the shore of life to the shore of death. Milan Kundera

Only at the last minute does he see it
the shining arc from dark to dark forever
himself upon it, weary beyond belief

and glad, to tell truth, that the day is over.
Tired and in pain he does not fear the good night
although he'd like to live a little longer

like Viscount Nelson, who knew it could not be.
In the victory of his own *Victory*,
his duty well performed, was that all there was?

4. A game of cards

Crossing the Golden Horn the British couple
ignore the spectacularly crippled Kurd
who begs baksheesh, showing off deformity,
his desperate livelihood and stock-in-trade,
to play the cards the way their friends invented.
This week in new Pera, next in old Stamboul,
by turn and turn about, cross the black water,
until kings, queens, knaves, aces – and the joker –
of diamonds, hearts, clubs, spades in red and black
become their bridge. To kill time, perhaps, or pain.

Part V

Bombers

Yes, I remember that sound, a throbbing roar
steady above the thunder of ack-ack and

crumps of bombs exploding on Merseyside docks
and how the sound infected the pure moonlight

with evil it never quite lost, not for me
or others who lived that shit and corruption.

or the mean rowhouses of Rugby and Crewe
Now the groundlings don't hear the bombers at all

cruising the high atmosphere like meteorites
they rush aloft too distant for sound or sight

until their blasting fires slash the tender earth
to blow away cities on a cloudless day.

Dracula verses

1. The governess

O you whose days have shrunk to disappointment
and you who are still far from worldly wisdom,
consider the charming inexperience
that makes romance plausible. She could be you.

Transportation is normally by shipwreck,
says Frye's excellent guidebook to this region.
Tower and battlements glower above her,
wolfpacks are howling from the windy forest.
A manservant opens the groaning portal,
on yawning glooms of vast halls and passages
and black shapes lurking among blacker shadows

The comfortable glow of a library.

2. The castle

For the house itself no precise plan exists
since no one has ever been in all the rooms.
Again, it changes from visit to visit
is accessible to view only in dreams
and never never explored in full daylight.
The great hall** is well worth a détour with its
minstrels' gallery and oriel window,
but its details are clear only when looked at
closely and on fresh inspection have shifted.
The numberless stairways, vaguely like those in
Piranesi's *Imaginary Prisons*
also change subtly on closer scrutiny.
There are dungeons and laboratories in
the crypt, and an extensive torture chamber***
fitted with immense terrifying engines.

Somewhere far down a river runs underground
which floods occasionally, tumbling the house
in fungus spotted ruins, though all's renewed
at the next creation. Labyrinthine caves
accommodate the excellent cellars whose
casks and bottles decant vintage wine and blood.
Certain monsters, home made, misbegotten or
trapped are chained here to howl their incessant pain.
Relatives who are merely insane are caged
in towers and attics, attended by keepers.
By the way service here is slow, and the food
displays a certain sombre *je ne sais quoi.*

The chapel* contains a fine baroque organ
with some unusual features of its own;
in addition to three manuals there are
two pedal-boards (for quadruped organists)
and unique stops such as *vox demonica.*
There is also a busy mausoleum**.
The grand staircase with its armorial beasts
is unfrequented; denizens elect
to use the secret passages and stairways,
vanishing through stone walls, bookcases, panels,
dissolving mirrors, trapdoors, chimney pieces.
Bedrooms: many guests prefer to bring their own,
though subject here to disquieting changes.
The same visitors close down most of the house
and use two or three rooms, too mean-spirited
to inhabit the more spacious life of the dream.
A lead tub, cased in polished mahogany,
distinguishes the main bathroom**; the waste pipe
domiciles a black scorpion who scuttles out
when the taps spurt brown water and scalding steam.
The throne is also mahogany, the bowl
is an original by Thomas Crapper.
A shelf of reading matter is provided.
the *Report of the Imperial Royal
Commission on Lycanthropy*, twelve volumes;
back numbers of obsolete magazines like
The New York Review of Haematophagy.
No one has ever read these publications.

The Castle has many personalities,
plays a part in the story, or not, at will,
utters secrets, takes due notice of questions
and tries to take a responsible stand on
the Great Issues, without loss of mystery.
'We try to take a responsible stand on
the Great Issues, without loss of mystery,'
the Castle said today in a brief statement.

It is nothing if not accommodating.

3. Dinner à deux

She does like to see him in white tie and tails,
a bit of the richness and nothing but the best.
Formality is lovely when all else fails,
and what is that star glittering from his chest.

O she does like to wear her gilded sequins
and sip champagne demurely by candlelight
and hear the chat of one who often frequents
the best society, though a fly-by-night.

for the Great World is not far as the bat flies
and the blood of royal Europe's in his veins.
O what of his long fangs and those bright mad eyes?
Blood will tell, the mark of distinction remains.

She does like to taste spectacular dishes
while he drinks dark wine from his own decanter,
remarking how the servants jump at his wishes
when he snarls like a pedigree black panther.

'Little fool, little fool!' the butler hisses:
'You're heading for a fall!' (and try hissing that)
But she is dreaming of steaming hot kisses
and swooning under the moon and this and that

It is true that his manners are disgraceful
and that he seldom relinquishes his sneer.
The girl who took him on would have her plate full –
it's not so much that he's odd as that he's queer,

and true that pretty women can divert him,
make his lip curl at dinner-time without fail.
But this one is convinced she can convert him
though the only blood he's thristing for is male!

4. Dead end

He sleeps out the day in his lonely coffin;
she catches butterflies in her silken net,
transfixing each one with the stake of a pin
still murmuring the queer name she can't forget.

'O Count Dracula, what an old fag you are!
We could have been happy, my blush and your sneer.
My fudge melts when you growl like a jaguar,
but it's no good, you don't even know I'm here!'

5. *Resolution*

Infected by the virus of her vampire,
Missy will sing no more songs by the campfire;

On the other hand, she is now a countess
who has flown upstairs from her halfway downstairs

to take her place with the powers of the air
as Queen of the Night. The story leaves her there.

Part VI

Thanksgiving

I am afraid of this Indian summer:
this gentle light has the finality of
a sunrise seen while smoking the last cigarette
before the bullet in the neck. The condemned
are treated with tender consideration
which only tends to fearful premonition.
The hand trembles accepting this late garland
in the untrustworthy sunlight of the fall.

There have been omens, old men saying goodbye,
a book falling, a black dog on the sidewalk,
a sudden chill where no wind stirred in the leaves.
I take this happiness for a parting gift.

The dear ruin

The girl must be out of her mind – she insists
it's this ruin of a body she's after.
Impossible! though I long to believe her
and maybe could if I kept clear of mirrors.
So Marilyn must have felt when Arthur breathed,
It's your wonderful mind I'm crazy about.

Enigma

Beauty of landscapes where men have left no trace,
Even the importunate wind asks no promises!
And woman wailing for her hairy lover:
Romantic dream to marry an angel.

Forgotten

What I remember about the woman is
her big Dutch feet with which she could field golfballs,

thread needles, open beer bottles, play the harp
or tug at your zipper under the table.

Hands busy with phone and notebook she would sit
wringing in agitation those clever feet;

sometimes, disguised as a pioneer granny
in print flounces, she would stuff the feet into
huge cowboy boots and trample on her lovers.

O word of fear

She keeps another man at home, I'm afraid,
who waters her plants and helps with the mortgage.
Him she keeps warm and balances his diet.
Devil send him a long standing on weak legs!
And yet, why should I wish him harm, the creature,
who remains after all only a husband
who figures in her plans. It is in her dreams
I figure, if at all. So who is the cuckold?

Public appeal

I call upon the striking electricians
who keep the municipal library closed
to consider their brother and well-wisher –
not that I use the place, but her husband does.
Anything that takes the good man's mind off books
is bad and positively not to be brooked.
He'll be hanging round the house next and, who knows?
may try catching up on his domestic chores.
Back to work brothers, lights on, open the doors!

Parting

No, you never deceived me; you said nothing
and did not look at me as you came to bed.
Later, a child leaving a birthday party,
you murmured Thank you I had a lovely time.

The room you left that morning is still empty.

The bionic woman

'The much-maligned, often unreliable',
and 'sometimes magnificent male appendge,
root of our pain and pleasure and life itself,'
said the front cover of Cosmo magazine
announcing an article we did not read,
assuming, no doubt on the best evidence,
the root can no longer stand up for itself.

We may take judicial notice of 'maligned'
and call no further evidnece on that point.
Unreliable? So Ovid testifies,
and Boswell and others, not all so famous.
This is, by the way, a divine attribute
reminding us again that love is a god
not to be compelled, even by ritual.
Most texts assume a priapic readiness
in men, and in women a common reluctance
demanding something called 'sexual technique',
poetry, flowers, encouraging speeches.
Coition, thus, is something he does to her,
not she with him; thus 'root' becomes 'appendage'
whose absence is scarcely missed or regretted
when female seeks her jollies in solitude
with the far more reliable vibrator.
The bionic woman, all volts and switches,
needs to blow her pretty fuses now and then.

Safari

At the trail's end is a river still to cross,
verdigris on copper, green smudge on burnt plain,
where trees send roots to drink life from the flood.
Descend by elephant tracks to the cold brink
where the wrinkled elder waits with his dugout
to ferry hunters over the fast torrent
to the farther shore, grassy and cool for rest.
From there to the blue mountains teeming with game
is a day's march, no more. And there it begins.

One more safari in that country I'll make
and ferry over the dangerous river
with the elder, who still knows me and takes his coins.
And when I gain the foothills I'll rest a while.

The cardinal at luncheon

When a Frenchman kisses his fingers like this
He's thinking about food, says his Eminence.
When we Italians, however, do it
It is to salute some beautiful woman.
Alas, I myself may not make such gestures.

God has rewarded him with a sound liver
And a spongy prostate ripe for the surgeon.

Pilate washing his hands

I do what I can. I make no promises
My hands are tied. I have no authority.
There are certain procedures, certain guidelines.
I don't make the rules. I'm just doing my job.

Don't talk to me, I only run this outfit.
Nobody tells me anything around here.
I'm the last person to hear what's going on.
What do I have to do to get some action.

I'd count to five on this one if I were you.
The important thing is not what I think but what you think.

Before I answer, let me explain something.
I am simply the servant of the people.

Madam tells all

I am telling my secrets before I die.
come closer. Listen, this is a confession.
I can name the man who stole the crown jewels
under the noses of the castle heralds–
O yes, the old king of arms was suspected,
someone killed him later, during the Troubles.
I know about that too and will disclose all,
but that is not what I meant to tell you about.
What does it matter now? a few diamonds!
Listen, I was with Adolf when he, when he –
that does not matter either, the man was mad.
What I meant, what I really meant to say was
I am telling my secrets before I die.
Start the tape now, here was this head of state
between my – ah, a silver-tongued spellbinder
jawing insanely, and all for my pleasure,
till once I nabbed him, still giving tongue of course,
catching Watergate on TV with one eye.
I am selling his secrets before I die.

Perils and dangers

What if the engines failed just after takeoff,
What if the road fell away under our wheels,
What would you do if your partner should make off
With every cent you own? You'd know how it feels
If all were as dicey as scripture reveals.

True, there's little enough for faith to go on
And no incantation can cause it to grow
Sun rises and sets, moon follows, and so on,
Faith, our human bond, is placed in what we know.

The road

To quit the warm bed and step into the cold
To leave sunlit paths and walk the rainy road

To forsake good company and go alone
Not to rest, but to travel in the dark zone

To be poor though a king, wise in foolishness
Like hopeless love, pilgrims call it happiness

Old man's song

Yes, I am sick and my sickness is called life.
too much of it can be dangerous to health
and maybe I have, as they say, overdosed.
Meanwhile coconut palms are not far away
along a coral shore where waves bang all day.
The suns arc over forever and return
and I am grateful, of course, for your concern.

Benediction

Eleven blessings attend this little book
including a secret one, never disclosed:
the hand that touches it, that hand shall be filled;
the eye that reads it, that eye shall be lustrous;
the mouth that cites it, that mouth shall be honeyed;
the ear that hears it, that ear shall be music-filled;
the mind that takes it, that mind shall be wakened;
the heart that keeps it, that heart shall be leaping;
the shop in which it is sold shall gain profits;
the bed in which it is read shall be fruitful;
who reads this book, his sins shall be forgiven;
and she that buys shall have wisdom, health and love.

• Cap-Saint-Ignace
• Sainte-Marie (Beauce)
Québec, Canada
1997